Mis, Melody S.

How to draw Pennsylvania's sights
and symbols

A Kid's Guide to Drawing America™

How to Draw
Pennsylvania's
Sights and Symbols

Melody S. Mis

The Rosen Publishing Group's
PowerKids Press™
New York

To my mother, Liberty "Libby" Mis Nagle, whose name reflected her independent spirit

Published in 2002 by The Rosen Publishing Group, Inc.
29 East 21st Street, New York, NY 10010

First Edition

Editor: Jannell Khu
Book Design: Kim Sonsky
Layout Design: Colin Dizengoff

Illustration Credits: Laura Murawski
Photo Credits: pp. 7, 22 © Bettmann/CORBIS; p. 8 © *Portrait of William Trost Richards, ca. 1890.* Photographs of Artists - Collection I, Archives of American Art, Smithsonian Institution; p. 9 © Collection of Brandywine River Museum, purchased through a grant from the Pew Memorial Trust; pp. 12, 14 © One Mile Up, Incorporated; p. 16 © Hal Horwitz/CORBIS; p. 18 © Kennan Ward/CORBIS; p. 20 © David Muench/CORBIS; p. 24 © Peter Finger/CORBIS; p. 26 © Stuart Westmorland/CORBIS; p. 28 © Index Stock.

Mis, Melody S.
How to draw Pennsylvania's sights and symbols / Melody S. Mis.
p. cm. — (A kid's guide to drawing America)
Includes index.
Summary: This book explains how to draw some of Pennsylvania's sights and symbols, including the state seal, the official flower, and the Liberty Bell.
  ISBN 0-8239-6094-3
1. Emblems, State—Pennsylvania—Juvenile literature 2. Pennsylvania—In art—Juvenile literature   3. Drawing—Technique—Juvenile literature   [1. Emblems, State—Pennsylvania 2. Pennsylvania   3. Drawing—Technique]
I. Title II. Series
  2002
  743'.8'99748—dc21

Manufactured in the United States of America

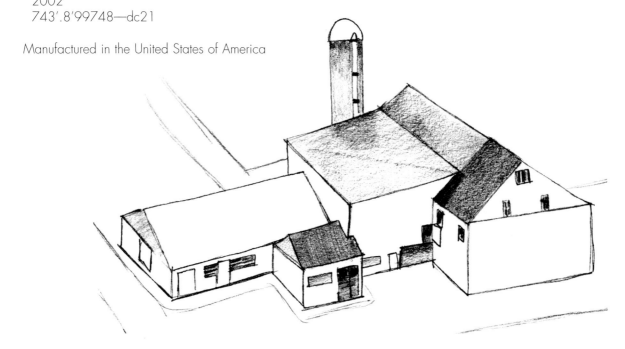

CONTENTS

Let's Draw Pennsylvania

Pennsylvania's capital city is Harrisburg, and its most populated city is Philadelphia with 1,478,000 residents. Philadelphia means "city of brotherly love" in Greek. Pittsburgh's iron and steel industry added to the growth of Pennsylvania's economy during the nineteenth century. Industrial giants such as Andrew Carnegie and Thomas Mellon built their steel empires in Pittsburgh. One of the state's professional football team is named the Pittsburgh Steelers!

Pennsylvania is home to many companies that produce snack foods. In fact Hershey, Pennsylvania, was built around the chocolate industry! The town is named after Pennsylvania native Milton Hershey. In 1905, he opened the world's largest chocolate factory, which is known today as Hershey Foods Corporation. Today Hershey is one of Pennsylvania's major tourist attractions. Visitors can see how chocolate is made, can sample chocolates made by the company, and can even walk under street lamps that are shaped like Hershey's chocolate kisses!

One important tourist attraction in Pennsylvania is

Valley Forge. This place was the home for General George Washington's Continental army during the winter of 1777–1778. During the cold winter months, many soldiers died of hunger and sickness. The soldiers who survived spent the winter training for battle. These soldiers helped America win the American Revolution (1775–1783).

To draw some of Pennsylvania's sights and symbols, you start with one shape and add other shapes to it. New steps are shown in red. Directions are under each step. Gather the following supplies to draw Pennsylvania's sights and symbols:

- A sketch pad
- An eraser
- A number 2 pencil
- A pencil sharpener

These are some of the shapes and drawing terms you need to know to draw Pennsylvania's sights and symbols:

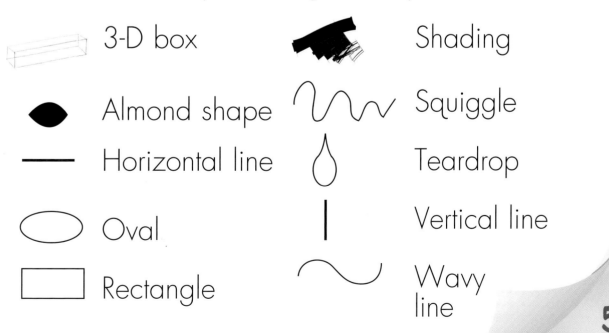

3-D box		Shading	
Almond shape		Squiggle	
Horizontal line		Teardrop	
Oval		Vertical line	
Rectangle		Wavy line	

The Keystone State

Pennsylvania was nicknamed the Keystone State in the early 1800s. In architecture a keystone is a wedge-shaped stone in an arch that holds all the other stones together. Pennsylvania was compared to a keystone because it is located in the middle of America's original 13 colonies. Its location made Pennsylvania a key state for trading. Trade was important to Pennsylvania's economy.

Pennsylvania's other nickname is the Quaker State. William Penn (1644–1718) was the founder of Pennsylvania. He lived in England and belonged to a religious group called the Quakers. Penn preached and wrote about the Quakers' beliefs. The Quakers were persecuted in England. Penn wanted a safe place for Quakers to live and to worship in peace. In 1681, King Charles II of England gave Penn a large piece of land in the New World. People called America the New World then. Pennsylvania was named in honor of William Penn's father. Pennsylvania means "Penn's woods."

In 1682, Quaker leader William Penn arrived in the area that would later become Pennsylvania. The Quakers were the first people from Europe to settle this area. Pennsylvania's nickname the Quaker State honors these first settlers.

7

Pennsylvania Artist

William Trost Richards

William Trost Richards was born in Philadelphia, Pennsylvania, in 1833, to a Quaker family. Before Richards painted professionally, he illustrated and designed ornamental metalwork for a company that produced gas lamps. Drawing pictures of fixtures sharpened Richards's natural artistic talents and honed his attention to detail. These are skills that he later applied to painting. In 1852, one of his landscape paintings was accepted and was shown by the Pennsylvania Academy of the Fine Arts in Philadelphia. The following year, after three more paintings were shown, Richards was encouraged to pursue an art career.

In 1862, Richards and his artist friends formed an organization called the Society for the Advancement of Truth in Art. This organization was modeled after the Pre-Raphaelite movement of painting. This movement was formed in the mid-1800s by young English artists. One aspect of Pre-Raphaelite art that appealed to

Richards was that it stressed the importance of paying close attention to detail and color. Richards was one of the most detail-oriented artists of his generation. Richards's skill in capturing the details and the natural lighting of a landscape is shown in his painting *The Valley of the Brandywine, Chester County (September [?])*. It takes a great amount of talent, skill, patience, and time to capture a landscape so accurately that the finished work looks like a photograph! Richards settled in Germantown, Pennsylvania, and died in 1905.

Richards painted *The Valley of the Brandywine, Chester County (September [?])* around 1886–1887. It was done in oil on canvas and measures 44" x 55" (112 cm x 140 cm). During the 19th century, many American landscape artists came to Chester County, Pennsylvania, to paint the beautiful Brandywine Valley.

Map of Pennsylvania

Map of the Continental United States

The three major rivers in Pennsylvania are the Delaware, the Susquehanna, and the Ohio Rivers. The Allegheny and the Pocono mountain ranges are in the northern and the western parts of the state. They are part of the Appalachian Plateau, which runs from New York to Alabama. Coal and oil are natural resources found in the Appalachian Plateau. The state's highest point is Mount Davis at 3,213 feet (979 m). The Great Valley and Piedmont regions consist of mountain ridges and rolling plains. They are located in eastern Pennsylvania. Some of America's richest farmland is located in the fertile valleys of the Piedmont area. The Erie Lowlands are in the western part of Pennsylvania. They border Lake Erie, one of the five Great Lakes.

1

Draw a rectangle. Notice the small bump on the top left side. Next draw two pointed shapes to the right side of the rectangle as shown.

2

Soften and shape the right side so it looks like the above. Erase extra lines. Draw a five-pointed star for the capital, Harrisburg.

3

Draw a circle within a circle for the city of Philadelphia.

4

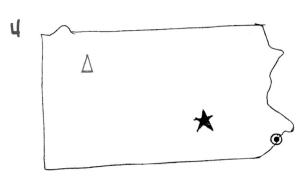

Draw a triangle for the Allegheny National Forest.

5

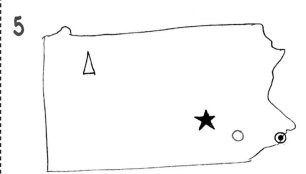

Draw a circle for Lancaster County.

6

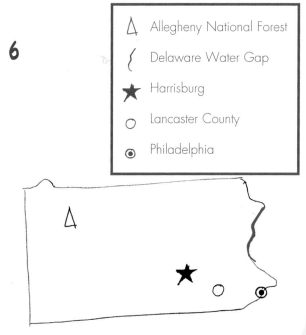

△	Allegheny National Forest
{	Delaware Water Gap
★	Harrisburg
○	Lancaster County
◉	Philadelphia

Draw a curved line on the right side of the state for the Delaware Water Gap. You can also draw the map key.

The State Seal

Pennsylvania's state seal was approved by the state legislature in 1791. A shield is in the center of the seal. The shield is divided into three sections. A sailing ship is in the top section. It stands for trade. Ships moved products to and from America using Pennsylvania's ports. A plow is in the middle section. It stands for the importance of farming to Pennsylvania's economy. Three bundles of wheat are in the bottom section. They stand for agriculture.

On top of the shield is an eagle. The eagle is America's symbol for freedom. A stalk of Indian corn is on the left of the shield. It represents agricultural wealth. On the right of the shield is an olive branch. It is a symbol of peace. The words "Seal of the State of Pennsylvania" appear around the seal.

1

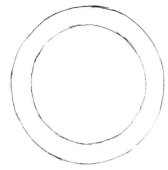

Draw a circle. You can trace around a jar lid. Draw another circle inside the first one.

2

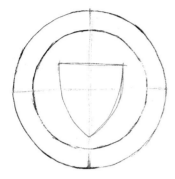

Lightly draw a vertical line and a horizontal line through the center of the two circles. Use the lines as guides and draw a shield in the center of the inner circle.

3

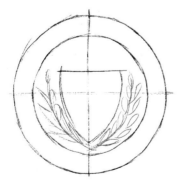

Draw a curved line on either side of the shield. These are the branches. Draw little leaves on either side of the lines.

4

Draw the bald eagle on top of the shield.

5

Make the top of the shield into a curved line. Divide the shield into three sections. Draw a ship on top, a plow in the center, and three bundles of wheat on the bottom. Shade in the leaves and the eagle.

6

Erase extra lines. Write "SEAL OF THE STATE OF PENNSYLVANIA" in the outer circle. Draw the flowery design at the bottom using wavy lines.

The State Flag

Pennsylvania adopted its state flag in 1907. The flag's field is blue, the same blue that is used in the flag of the United States. In the center of the flag is the state's coat of arms. The same images found in the seal are featured in the coat of arms. There is a black horse on either side of the coat of arms. The horses stand for power. The design of the horses was changed several times. In one design, the horses were white. In another design, both horses were lying down. Finally, in 1875, the Pennsylvania assembly voted to have black horses standing on their hind legs and facing each other. Placed under the horses is a red ribbon. The state's motto, Virtue, Liberty And Independence, is written on the ribbon.

1

Draw a rectangle. This is the basic shape of the flag.

2

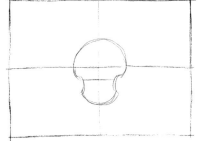

Draw a horizontal line and a vertical line through the center of the rectangle. Next draw the shape in the center. This is the shield.

3

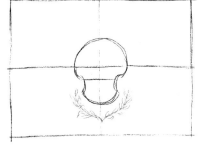

To draw the design below the shield, draw two curved lines. Next draw the oval-shaped leaves.

4

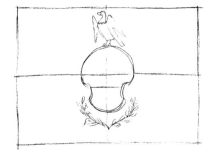

To draw the eagle, study the shape before you start. Break down the eagle into basic shapes, and draw them one shape at a time. For instance first draw a rectangle for the eagle's body. Then draw its beak, head, neck, and wings. Draw its legs last. Erase extra lines.

5

Draw the horse. Break down the horse into basic shapes, and draw them one at a time.

6

Draw the horse on the right side.

7

Draw the ribbon on the bottom.

8

Erase extra lines. Divide the shield into three sections. Draw the ship on the top, the plow in the middle, and the three bundles of wheat on the bottom. Draw two lines under the shield, and draw oval-shaped leaves. Shade your drawing, and you are done!

The Mountain Laurel

The mountain laurel became Pennsylvania's state flower in 1933. The mountain laurel is so popular that the city of Wellsboro holds the Pennsylvania State Laurel Festival every June. The flowers of the mountain laurel grow in clusters. The pink flowers add color to Pennsylvania's forests and mountainsides in the spring. The mountain laurel is a shrub. A shrub is a bush with branches that grow near the ground. It is smaller than a tree. The mountain laurel grows best in the mild climate and the moist soil of Pennsylvania's mountainous regions. It can grow to be 15 feet (4.5 m) tall, but it is usually about 3 feet (1 m) tall. The flowers of the mountain laurel are very pretty, but do not eat them. They are poisonous!

1

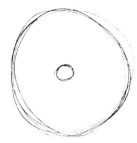

Draw a large circle. This is the basic shape of the flower. Draw another smaller circle in the center. This is the bud.

2

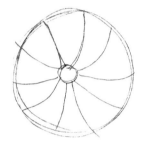

Draw lines that fan out from the center circle. Notice that it looks like a striped peppermint candy.

3

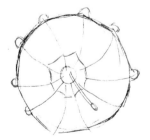

Draw a thin, matchlike shape in the center of the flower. Draw an outer circle around the center small circle. Notice that this circle looks like the top of an open umbrella. Now draw small half circles outside the biggest circle.

4

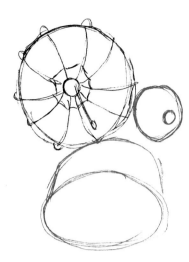

Below the first flower, draw a large oval. On top of this oval, draw a half circle as shown. On the right side, draw a small circle. Draw a smaller circle inside the one you just drew.

5

Draw in the curved lines on the two flowers as shown.

The Ruffed Grouse

The ruffed grouse became Pennsylvania's state bird in 1931. The ruffed grouse is also called a partridge or a pheasant. It is found in the northeastern United States. The adult ruffed grouse is from 16 to 19 inches (41–48 cm) tall. It is brown or gray and white with black markings on its neck

and tail. The ruffed grouse spends most of its time on the ground, but it can fly. When it sees an enemy, the grouse runs and makes a loud, whirring sound with its wings. Then it flies away. Enemies of the ruffed grouse include hawks, raccoons, and humans. People hunt the ruffed grouse for food. In the spring the male ruffed grouse attracts females by flapping its wings. The flapping makes a very loud noise. This is called drumming.

1

Draw a circle for the head. Draw an oval. This is the body.

2

Connect the two shapes with lines. This is the basic shape of the grouse.

3

Draw a small circle for the eye. Draw a sideways triangle for the beak. Lightly sketch the wings, and shape the tail feathers.

4

Draw the short legs and the claws.

5

Shade in the drawing. Turn your pencil on its side and begin shading lightly. When you shade, press down hard in some areas and lightly in others.

The Eastern Hemlock

Pennsylvania adopted the eastern hemlock as its state tree in 1931. This tree was chosen for several reasons. The hemlock is found in Pennsylvania's forests. It provides animals with food and shelter. Its lumber was used to build homes for early Pennsylvania pioneers. The eastern hemlock is an evergreen tree. Evergreen trees have foliage that remains green throughout the year. The eastern hemlock can grow to be 80 feet (24 m) tall. Its branches are covered with flat, green needles. This tree grows in the eastern half of the United States. It grows throughout Pennsylvania, but it grows best in the moist, cool weather of the state's mountains. The eastern hemlock is a hardy tree. It can live up to 1,000 years!

1

Draw three vertical lines. This is the trunk of the tree.

2

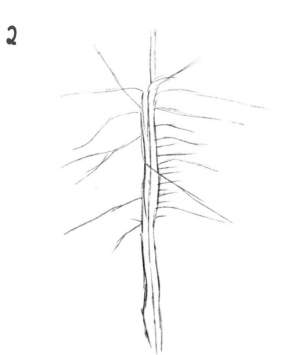

Draw lines that extend from the trunk. These are the branches. The branches do not have to be perfectly straight.

3

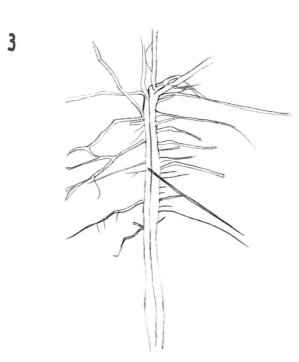

To make the branches thicker, draw other lines next to the first ones you drew for all the branches.

4

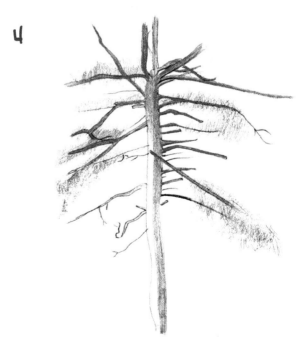

Shade in the drawing. Turn your pencil on its side and gently shade. Excellent job!

The Liberty Bell

In 1751, a foundry in England made a bronze bell for the state house, now called Independence Hall, in Philadelphia. The Declaration of Independence and the U.S. Constitution were written and were signed in Independence Hall. The bell cracked the first time it rang. In 1753, the bell was melted down and was recast. It cracked again! The bell was rung on July 8, 1776, to call people to the first public reading of the Declaration of Independence. The name Liberty Bell was first used in 1837, in a poem called "The Liberty Bell." The poem was published in a pamphlet that condemned slavery. In 1837, the country was divided on the practice of slavery. Antislavery groups and slaves saw the Liberty Bell as a symbol of freedom. The last time the bell rang was in 1846, to honor the first president, George Washington. In 1976, the Liberty Bell was moved to a park across from Independence Hall. You can see the Liberty Bell in its glass-walled structure.

1

Draw a rectangle. Next draw a horizontal line toward the top.

2

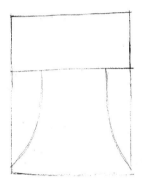

Draw two curved vertical lines. You just drew the basic shape of the Liberty Bell.

3

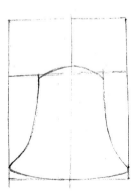

Lightly draw a vertical line through the center of the bell. You will use this as a guide in the next steps. Shape the top and the bottom of the bell with curved lines. Nice job!

4

Study the shapes shown in red before you start. Carefully draw one shape at a time. The shapes above consist of circles, lines, and rectangles.

5

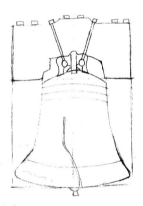

Draw six small rectangles above the bell. Next draw three horizontal lines in the upper part of the bell, and another one toward the bottom. Draw the bell's crack and its ringer.

6

Shade the drawing. Turn your pencil on its side and gently shade with side-to-side strokes. Erase extra lines.

23

The Amish

In the sixteenth century, new branches of the Protestant religion developed in Europe. The Mennonite religion  was one such branch. A Mennonite bishop, Jacob Amman, thought people should follow the Bible more strictly. He broke away from the Mennonites. People who followed Amman were called Amish.

In the early 1700s, many Amish moved to Lancaster County, Pennsylvania, and farmed. Amish farms are some of the most well kept and productive farms in the nation. The Amish live simply and do not believe in modern conveniences. Inside an Amish house, you won't find telephones, electricity, or televisions. They use wood-burning stoves to cook and to heat the house. They try to make many of the things they need, such as their clothes and furniture. With the help of their Amish community, some even build their own houses!

Draw a 3-D house shape. Draw the two rectangles on the bottom. Next draw the triangle on top. Finish with another rectangle top next to the triangle.

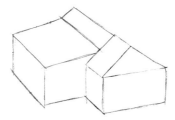

Draw a 3-D addition to the house. Draw the two bottom shapes first. Then draw the middle rectangle, and finish with the thinner rectangle.

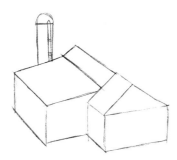

Draw a tall shape behind the house. Top this shape with a half circle. Draw lines inside this shape.

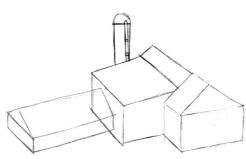

Next draw a long 3-D house shape. Draw the base first, which is the rectangle. Then draw the triangle on top.

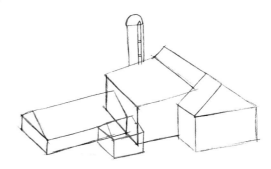

Draw another house shape next to the one you just drew. Notice how the right side extends over the rectangle.

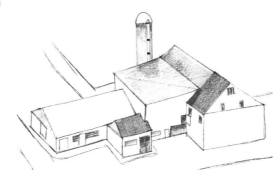

Draw the windows and the doors. Shade in the drawing. Turn your pencil on its side, and begin shading the tops of the houses and the rectangles lightly.

Pennsylvania Monument at Gettysburg

The Battle of Gettysburg took place in Pennsylvania. The three-day battle began on July 1, 1863. It was the Civil War's bloodiest battle. Nearly 50,000 men died. After the war, the battlefield was kept as a historic site. Union and Confederate states that were involved in this battle built monuments on the battlefield to honor their soldiers. Completed in 1913, Pennsylvania's monument is the largest. It honors the 34,000 Pennsylvanians who fought at Gettysburg. On each side of the monument is an arch that stands for victory. Above the arches, there are battle scenes carved into granite. Eight statues are placed around the monument. The statues include President Abraham Lincoln and Union general David Birney.

1

Draw a 3-D rectangle. Here's a hint, you will need to draw eleven lines.

2

Draw vertical lines that extend from the bottom of the rectangle. Connect those lines with slightly angled horizontal lines.

3

Erase extra lines. Draw three curved lines on top. Next draw a dome shape on top of the three curved lines you just drew.

4

Draw the lines as shown above.

5

On top of the building, draw lines parallel to the ones you drew in the last step. Next draw vertical lines for the columns.

6

Draw curved lines between the columns for the arches. Draw vertical and horizontal lines underneath the columns.

7

Draw curved lines inside the dome. On top of dome, draw the small shapes that the angel will stand on. Draw the angel with the sword.

8

Draw the steps. Shade the drawing and you're done!

27

Pennsylvania's Capitol

The first capitol in Harrisburg, Pennsylvania, was destroyed by fire in 1897. It was replaced with a plain brick building. In 1901, Joseph Huston, a Philadelphia architect, designed a new capitol. Completed in 1906, Huston built the capitol in the Italian Renaissance style. This style stresses that all sides of a building must be equally balanced. Huston wanted to make the new capitol a work of art. He made the capitol's dome like the dome of St. Peter's Basilica in Rome, Italy. The marble staircase in the rotunda, or round dome, is like the one in the Paris Opera House in Paris, France. Huston hired artists and craftspeople to create mural paintings and sculptures that show Pennsylvania's history.

1

Draw a 3-D rectangle. You will draw nine lines. This is the front side of the building.

2

Draw a thin 3-D shape next to the rectangle.

3

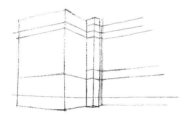

Draw lines as shown above. Notice the placement of these lines.

4

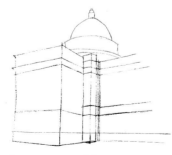

Now draw three curved lines on top of the building. Draw a semicircle above those lines. This is the dome. Draw little rectangles on top of the dome.

5

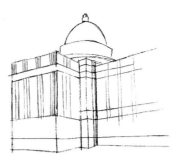

Draw vertical lines across the building as shown.

6

Draw horizontal lines on the top left side of the building. Add windows in the center of the building. Draw the doors on the bottom.

7

Draw lines inside the dome. Draw vertical lines under the dome for the columns. Draw in the trees by making fun shapes. Be creative with your shapes! Erase extra lines.

8

Shade in the drawing. Turn your pencil on its side and begin shading lightly. Notice how the trees are shaded the darkest. Excellent job!

Pennsylvania State Facts

Statehood	December 12, 1787, 2nd state
Area	46,058 square miles (119,290 sq km)
Population	12,281,100
Capital	Harrisburg, population, 50,900
Most Populated City	Philadelphia, population, 1,478,000
Industries	Steel, iron, coal, machinery, cement, food products
Agriculture	Dairy products, mushrooms, grains, tobacco, hogs, poultry
Animal	White-tailed deer
Beverage	Milk
Bird	Ruffed grouse
Flower	Mountain laurel
Fossil	Trilobite (hard-shelled sea creature)
Tree	Eastern hemlock
Fish	Brook trout
Insect	Firefly
Dog	Great Dane
Song	"Pennsylvania"
Motto	Virtue, Liberty And Independence
Nicknames	The Keystone State, The Quaker State

Glossary

American Revolution (uh-MER-uh-kenn reh-vuh-LOO-shun) Battles that soldiers from the colonies fought against England for freedom.

antislavery (an-tee-SLAY-vuh-ree) Against people "owning" other people as property.

bronze (BRONZ) A golden brown blend of copper and tin metals.

Civil War (SIH-vul-WOR) The war fought between the northern and southern states of America from 1861 to 1865.

coat of arms (KOHT UV ARMZ) A design on and around a shield or on a drawing of a shield.

Confederate (kuhn-FEH-duh-ret) Relating to the group of people who made up the Confederate States of America.

Continental army (kon-tin-EN-tul AR-mee) The army of patriots created in 1775 with George Washington as its commander in chief.

foliage (FOH-lee-ihj) Leaves, flowers, or branches of plants.

foundry (FOUN-dree) A place where metal is melted and is made into castings.

granite (GRA-niht) Melted rock that cooled and hardened beneath Earth's surface.

legislature (LEH-jihs-lay-cher) A body of people that has the power to make or pass laws.

mural (MYUR-ul) A picture painted on a wall or ceiling. A mural usually covers most of a wall.

ornamental (or-nuh-MEN-tuhl) Decorative.

pamphlet (PAM-flit) A small booklet with articles on a particular topic.

persecuted (PUR-suh-kyoot-ed) Treated cruelly because of one's race, religion, or political ideas.

plateau (pla-TOH) A flat area of land.

Protestant (PRAH-tes-tint) A Christian that does not belong to the Roman Catholic church.

Union (YOON-yun) The northern states that stayed loyal to the federal government during the Civil War.

Index

Web Sites

To learn more about Pennsylvania, check out these Web sites:
www.hersheypa.com/new_site/index.html
www.800padutch.com
www.ushistory.org/libertybell/index.html